Worlds Favorite Pets Pets in Every Home

Speedy Publishing LLC
40 E. Main St. #1156
Newark, DE 19711
www.speedypublishing.com

90% of pet owners
say they consider
their pet a member
of the family.

There is said to be around 400 million dogs in the world. Dogs have formed such a strong bond as pets, workers and companions to humans that they have earned the nickname man's best friend.

Cats are the most popular pet in the United States. Cats and humans have been associated for nearly 10000 years. Owning a cat can reduce the risk of stroke and heart attack by a third.

Hamsters have short tails, stout bodies, small ears, short legs, wide feet and large eyes. Hamsters are great as pets because they are easy to breed in captivity, easy to care for and interact well with people.

There are over 30000 known species of fish. There are hundreds of different kinds of fish that can be kept as pets. Fish tanks are really the best receptacles for keeping fish indoors.

Guinea pigs are very affectionate pets once they get to know and trust their owners. They are very social animals and they are much happier when kept in pairs or groups.

The parakeet is the most commonly kept bird in the world. Parakeets reproduce during the rainy season, when food is abundant.

Rabbits have a life expectancy of 9-10 years. Rabbits require a specialized diet that includes fresh fruits and vegetables.

9 7988 69 450326